For centuries juggling has been a performer's art. The trick of getting the three objects to dance around your hands has always managed to keep a small sense of magic about it.

Our purpose in writing *this* book however, is to take juggling off the stage and pass it around.

It is our belief that juggling really isn't a spectator sport.

It's one form of insanity we feel that everyone has a right to experience.

Juggling for the Complete Klutz

Juggling
for the
Complete
Klutz

By John Cassidy and B.C. Rimbeaux
Illustrated By Diane Waller

ISBN 0-932592-00-7

20th Printing, 1985

Second Edition

Printed in the United States of America

Published by
• Klutz Press •
Post Office Box 2992
Stanford, CA 94305

*Individual copies of this book
as well as assorted juggling equipment
may be ordered directly
from the publisher.
See back pages for details.*

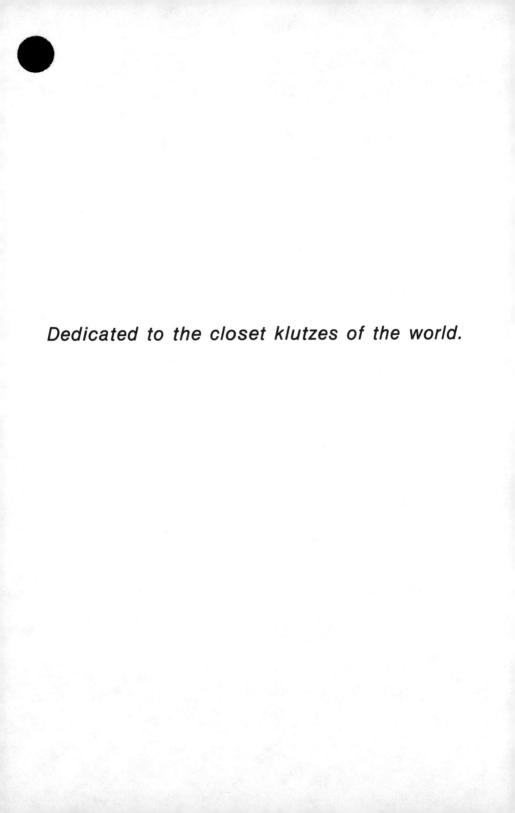

Dedicated to the closet klutzes of the world.

So you're interested in learning how to juggle but it took you four years to learn how to tie your shoes, and besides, dropping things has always been second nature to you. When your class played softball, you were always last picked and then packed off to right field. Your mother always puts away breakables whenever you step into the house. You're an original klutz and you probably think juggling is only for the super-coordinated.

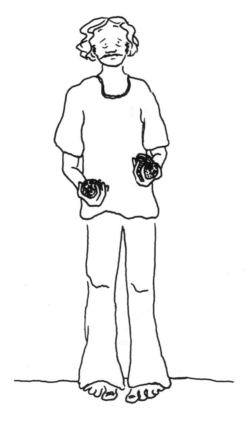

RELAX. Most people have got the moves down and are well on their way to juggling after only fifteen minutes, and even hard-core cases like you won't be far behind.

It's **SIMPLE!** The motions are new and for the first couple of minutes they feel as awkward as brushing your teeth left-handed, but the truth is — they're easy, and anyone can do it.

As for the question of Why? I can only mumble vaguely about the unknowable nooks and crannies of the human spirit. Or relate to you those times when I've found juggling to be just the answer for that slack moment or awkward minute. Perhaps you sometimes find yourself at a loss for a good "leave-'em-really-impressed" kind of parting line? At a job interview perhaps, or on a first date, what could be more appropriate? My own experience suggests that hitch-hiking may be the one arena where the juggler has a distinct advantage over his non-juggling competitor. Who could resist a little side-of-the-road razzle-dazzle?

Although the motions aren't difficult, they should be absorbed in bite-sized little chunks. Otherwise you'll run afoul of frustration, something that I will talk about a little later. In the meantime, read through the first three steps and glance at the pictures before picking up the bags. Don't bother reading about the problems just yet. They won't make sense until you have them anyway.

STEP I: The Drop

Pick up all three bags and hold them, briefly. You'll note that there is one more bag than you have hands, unless you are that rather rare case, in which event send away for our limited edition of *Juggling for the Exceptionally Gifted*.

Throw all three bags into the air and making no effort to catch any of them, let them all hit the ground. This is an example of **THE DROP.** I do it all the time and so will you, but it's good to familiarize yourself with the moves early on. Practice **THE DROP** until the novelty wears off. Many people find this occurs quite rapidly, others seem to get a lot out of this exercise for quite some time. Leaving those folks to themselves, we'll move on.

STEP II: The Toss

Put two bags away for a time and hold just one. Cradle it in the center of your hand, *not on your fingers.* (Read that last line again. It's more important than you think.)

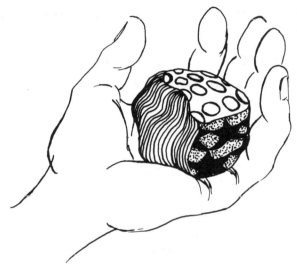

You should be standing, relaxed, even grinning perhaps, your elbows near your body and your hands at about waist height. Toss the bag in easy arcs about as high as your eyes and as wide as your body, back and forth, hand to hand. It won't take you long to discover that this exercise is only a hair more interesting than the first, but you should keep at it a little longer. The important thing is to keep your tosses consistent, one after the other, so that you don't have to go lunging around catching weird throws.

13

Don't make your throws stiffly either. Use a kind of "scooping" motion, as in the illustration. Ideally, you should be able to "scoop" a toss up and have it land — eyes closed — in your other hand. Realistically, if you can make the catch without having to dive for it, you'll be doing about normally.

Do this one until it gets boring. A minute seems to be about the limit for most people, but push yourself for a little more. Ignore those snickers from your audience, it's only the rawest kind of envy.

Figure 1: The "Scoop" Toss

STEP III: The Exchange

This is THE step, so pay attention. Read it all the way through before you do anything rash.

Pick up a second bag and cradle it in your hand so that you now have a bag in each hand. Look at *figure 2* for an idea of what's going to happen here. I'll try to explain at the same time by hitting some of the key points and then going over some of the common problems — but don't let all the coaching throw you. Remember, it's a new motion so it's awkward at first, but persevere.

Using your best STEP II toss, throw one bag up and over toward your other hand. Let it come to the top of its arc, and then, just as it starts to drop down into your other hand — which is holding the second bag — exchange the two, in one motion, by "scoop-tossing" the second and catching the first. Confusing, isn't it? But look at the pictures and keep reading.

The First Toss
Your hand should
move in a little
scooping motion.

a.

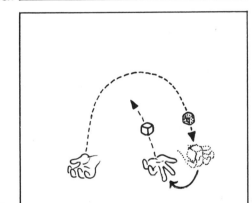

The Exchange
Your hand swings
in to make the
toss and out to
make the catch.

b.

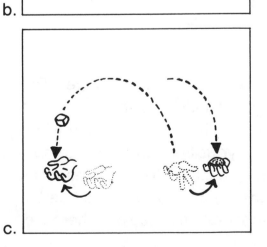

The Grand Finale

Figure 2

c.

Your second toss should pass to the inside of the first so that both throws ARE IN THE SAME PLANE RIGHT THERE IN FRONT OF YOU. Also, the path of the second toss should look the same as the first in terms of height and width. And remember, that second toss should not happen until the first has passed through the top of its arc. Otherwise, you will create all kinds of havoc. The exchange should be one smooth "scoop" toss-and-catch motion.

Figure 3

All right. That's the way it's supposed to happen. But go ahead and work at it for a little bit and then come back and I'll talk about how it *really* happened when you tried it. Incidentally, your first ten or so attempts are going to look and feel just terrible, so you might as well get used to that one right away. But take heart, a mere ten minutes or so generally makes a big difference.

You're back, right? And you've got some problems. I know the feeling well, but read on for help is on the way.

The most popular (and obnoxious) problem that confronts most ·people at this point is throwing the bags too far out in front of themselves, so that the second catch has to be made with a fully extended arm. In extreme cases, you'll find yourself making these frantic, diving grabs.

This is a very insidious problem and represents the biggest obstacle in learning to juggle. Fortunately there have been many here before you, so the path to salvation is well charted. So if you have it (and you probably do), read on. . . .

Stop everything for a minute and relax. This is actually a psychological hang-up that is caused by an undue amount of anxiety over that second toss. As the first throw is starting to drop in and your brain realizes that there's *already* a bag in the hand that's planning to make the catch, it flashes this panic signal down the line: "Get *rid* of that thing! Throw it *anywhere, but clear that hand!*", which results in a desperate heave putting the bag far out of your reach.

But now get a grip on yourself and concentrate on where you're going to put that second toss, and how you're going to throw it. It should pop out of the center of your hand and pass just to the *inside* of the first bag's arc. The two bags should pass one another about six inches above your hand. AND IT ALL HAPPENS IN A SINGLE, VERTICAL PLANE (check *figure 3* again).

You may find that all this concentration on your second toss makes you flub up the first catch. This is really a minor problem that will correct itself shortly. The crucial thing is to keep those tosses consistent and in the same plane — right there in front of you.

OK, enough words. Try it for another five minutes or so, making your first toss from your right hand... then five minutes with your first toss coming from your left. If it still feels just terrible, check out some of the helpful hints in STEP V: Special Problems.

STEP IV: The Jug

The hardest thing about STEP IV is knowing when to go for it. If you've got your exchanges down — in both hands — then this is just the wrap-up. So ask yourself if you're feeling pretty smooth before you jump into this one.

You are? Fine, you're home free. You may not have realized it, but you already know the basic juggling moves. So take a deep breath and pick up all three bags. Imagine for a moment how this amazing thing is going to look. Starting with your two-bag hand, you're going to give one of the bags a good toss and suddenly it'll be in the air, arching over toward your other hand. Meanwhile, you're still going to be holding one bag in each hand. Now as this flying bag begins to drop down into your hand, you should recognize a familiar scene. Exchange the flier with the held bag which then goes to the top of *its* arc, and as *it* starts to come in for a landing, you exchange *it* for the other held bag which then begins its little trip.

As you're doing this, it'll probably help to count out loud to yourself. Throwing the first bag up is "1", the second bag is "2", the third bag "3", and for the moment at least, that should be plenty.

Note: Just because I didn't put all the dotted hands in this illustration doesn't mean you should stop doing the "scoop-toss" thing. I just figured you'd gotten the point by now and besides, I didn't want to mess up the drawing.

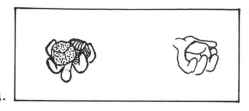

a.

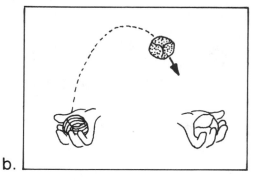

The First Toss

b.

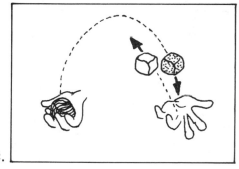

The First Exchange

c.

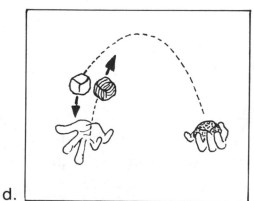

The Second Exchange
Note that your hands weave back and forth ("scoop tossing") so that the up-going bag can avoid the down-going one.

d.

If you can do this much, take a low bow. You're JUGGLING!!! All this time you thought juggling was keeping two or three things in the air at once. Now you should be able to see that there's really one *one* thing flying around — the others are just being held until they get exchanged with the flier, one at a time.

If you can put two exchanges back to back, I call that a "jug." Two jugs would be four exchanges in a row without a drop.

Once you can do a jug there'll be no stopping you. But let me explain what will undoubtedly start happening. In the heat of the moment you'll forget to concentrate on your tosses and they'll begin to fly out away from you, resulting in the "sprinting juggler syndrome."

When this starts to happen (and don't worry, it happens to everyone) remember what you learned about keeping your exchanges in one plane by tossing each bag to the *inside* of the dropping bag's arc. And don't start using your whole arm to make your tosses either. Keep your elbows pretty close to your sides and your hands at about waist height. Practice in front of a wall if you want, but......CONCENTRATE ON WHERE YOU'RE PUTTING THOSE TOSSES!

To continue on in this vein is to run the risk of becoming a nag. And so I will leave you with no more warning than this: take frequent breaks while you're trying to learn. Twenty minutes spent in two ten minute spurts is much more effective than in one lump.

And when all else fails, remember these few words whose wisdom has guided me through more than just a few trying times: "It's always darkest just before it gets pitch black."

STEP V: Special Problems

Most everyone seems to have a strong tendency to turn to this section too soon. Deep in our hearts we all figure we're exceptional — one way or another — and consequently deserving of some special attention.

It is often a deeply humbling experience to realize that our problems are neither very unusual, nor even very serious. So I will try to break this to you as gently as I can. If you've been trying for ten minutes or so and are still dropping a lot or having trouble keeping all the action right there in front of you (here it comes, so steel yourself), you're probably doing quite well — just suffering from a mild shortage of practice. Try it for a little longer and then take a break. You'll get less frustrated that way and it will give your muscles a chance to think about it all.

After a little while, pick up the bags and try it again with renewed concentration. If it still doesn't click at all, read on and see if you can recognize whatever it is that's holding you up.

PROBLEM: You're on STEP III: THE EXCHANGE, with just two bags, but you can't seem to make it work. You flub up the toss, you flub up the catch...everything feels terrible, and you've tried and tried.

BEST SOLUTION: Go get yourself a friend — you probably need one about now anyhow — and have him stand next to you, shoulder to shoulder. You can hold hands if you want, or if you're not that kind of friends, you can put your inside hands behind your own backs.

With your outside hands you're going to be doing exchanges. This is how it goes:

Put a bag in your outside hand and one in your friend's. Toss your bag in a nice easy arc over to your friend. Just before it lands in his hand (it's occupied, right?), he should toss you his bag and catch yours — all in that one hand, don't forget. His throw should go underneath yours. Doing exchanges like this (with two people) should slow things down enough so that you can eliminate the element of panic from your tosses. Change places with your friend after a little while so that you can loosen up both hands.

If you and your friend happen to be a particularly smooth team, you might want to extend this exercise into something that might be called "Siamese-twin" juggling. All you have to do is add a third bag to the act, which quickens things up a bit, but not too badly. Instead of doing one exchange and stopping, you're going to be doing a bunch of exchanges back-to-back (or side-to-side as the case happens to be).

If you can get some kind of blasé expression on your faces while you're doing this, then you've got your first trick — which isn't bad progress at all.

SECOND BEST SOLUTION
Since this is really just a psychological problem, there are a couple of possible psychological solutions.

One that I have used with some success is the idea of throwing the second bag through an imaginary wire loop "attached" to the dropping bag.

Try this for one or two exchanges. At the finish of each exchange, stop and ask yourself if your throw went through the "loop". If it didn't, ask yourself by how much you missed. If you can tell yourself how far off you were, then you've got your concentration focussed on the right place, i.e. the placement of that second toss.

Another use of the same idea is to paint little targets on the palms of your hands. This can make for awkward explanations during the non-juggling portion of your day though, and I offer it only as a suggestion.

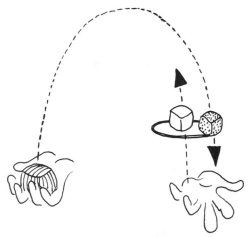

PROBLEM: You're on STEP IV: The Jug, and you are a serious sprinting juggler. There is no way you can keep your throws under control.

SOLUTION: First of all, practice in front of a wall so that you *can't* throw them too far out in front of you. An alternative to this: try it sitting down. (I've never found this to be so great, but everyone else says it helps, so I'll pass it on.) As a last resort you might try practicing on the edge of a cliff. A close friend of mine (rest his soul) used to swear by this one.

PROBLEM: Your legs are killing you from picking up your drops all the time.

SOLUTION: Stand over a table, hire a bag boy, *OR* BUILD YOUR OWN RETRIEVAL SKIRT (see picture for construction details).

Once you've smoothed out your three-bag juggling and can do it without having to dash across the room, you'll probably start wondering about the next step. Your friends, too, will be getting bored with your new little act. "What about four?" they'll ask innocently. Or even better, "How many can you do?" as if anything less than eleven would put them to sleep.

Juggling is not a spectator sport! If you want to be rid of these ingrates who don't know real talent when they see it, your only recourse is to stop juggling, hand them a bag and show them how to do THE TOSS. They'll be hooked in no time.

And once they are, you've got your partner for team juggling, which probably ought to be your first trick on your way to Ringling Brothers.

STEALING

You and your partner both ought to be at least fairly decent jugglers before you try this one. By that I mean you should each be able to do twenty or more jugs without dropping.

The ingredients for this trick are: two people and three juggling bags.

Let your partner begin this one. As he juggles merrily away, stand right beside him shoulder to shoulder, at the ready. For the first few attempts, this by itself will make him nervous enough to drop everything in hysterics. Once you've matured your way over that little hurdle, you can go on.

What you are going to do here is interrupt his juggling by taking two **successive** throws—one right after the other—just as they reach the tops of their arcs. That should leave you holding two bags. If your partner is cooperating, he can direct that third bag over your way. As it starts to drop into one of your (occupied) hands, just do an exchange—and you're off on your own, juggling away.

Be sure to start by taking a toss that comes out of your friend's outside hand with *your* outside hand. Then, on the very next toss, with your inside hand take the next bag (at the top of its arc), which should have come out of your friend's inside hand. As you're picking these bags off at the tops of their arcs, try to keep your palms up—you're catching these bags, not clawing them out of the air.

I realize this all sounds very complicated, but look at the diagrams and give it a try anyhow. Some things are a lot easier done than said.

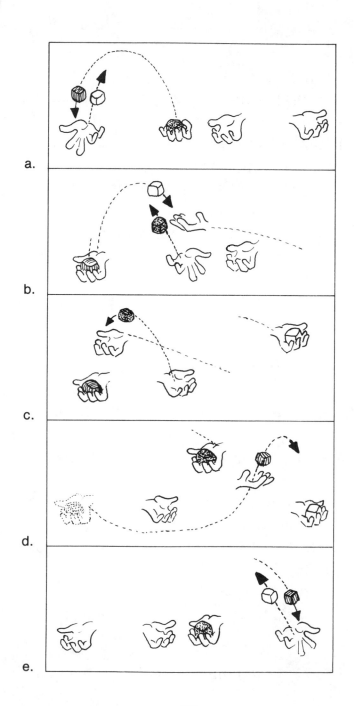

PASSING

This is the basic part of team juggling and it requires two pretty smooth jugglers. In other words, each of you ought to be able to do thirty or more jugs without a drop and still maintain a relatively calm expression on your faces.

Ingredients: two of the aforementioned type jugglers, and six bean bags.

Arrange yourselves so that you're facing each other, a few feet apart. In your right hands put two bags, in your lefts, one. Each of you start juggling, but make an effort to start together and stay in time—in other words, synchronously. It helps a lot if one of you counts out loud every time a toss leaves your right hand, "1...2...3".

OK. On a pre-arranged number, say three, instead of tossing across to your *own* left hand, throw your bag in a nice, easy arc, over to your friend's *left* hand. And at the same time, he should be doing exactly the same thing.

If it works out, (and it won't for a while), both of you will juggle along, switch two bags, and continue juggling—all without really missing a beat.

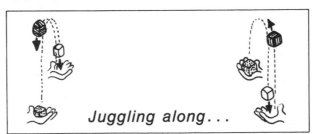

a.   *Juggling along...*

36

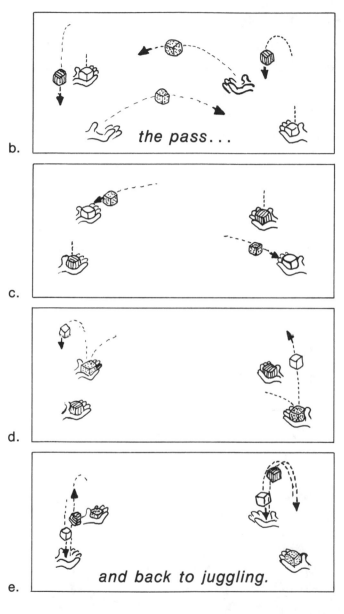

b. *the pass...*

c.

d.

e. *and back to juggling.*

It sounds tricky because it is, but there are a few warm-up exercises that can help.

Warm-up Exercise No. 1 While you're holding a bag in each hand, have your friend toss you a third — into your left hand. Before it lands, do an exchange and begin your own juggling. After a few moments juggling on your own, throw him one back — from your right hand — and stop.

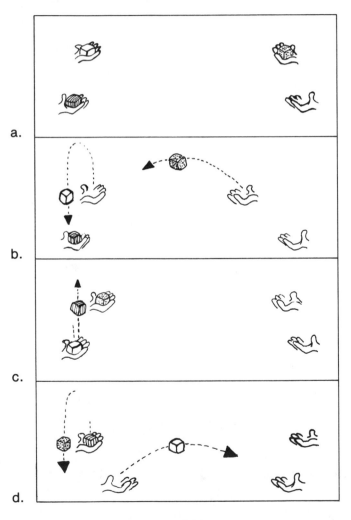

a.

b.

c.

d.

Warm-up Exercise No. 2 Start by holding three bags and giving your friend a fourth. Begin juggling (and counting) and then, on "three", make the toss over to your friend who — at the same time — should feed your hand with a nice easy toss. Your friend won't be juggling during this exercise. His job is strictly to catch your one toss while feeding you another. If it's done smoothly, you can juggle along without missing a beat.

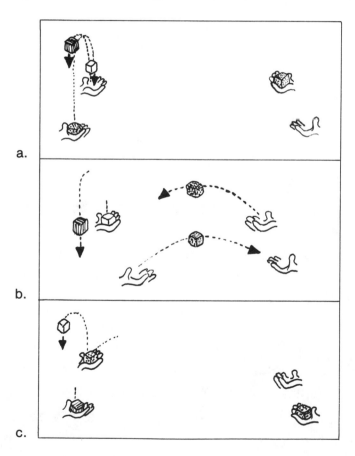

a.

b.

c.

Switch back and forth on all these exercises so that both of you can get it at the same time.

When you're by yourself, you can practice passing by standing in front of a wall and bouncing every third toss out of your right hand off the wall and into your left.

Just so you don't feel unusually handicapped, I'll describe the major problem that seems to get everyone when they try passing for the first time.

You'll be juggling along, both of you in time. On the third throw out of your right hand, you'll do it just the way you're supposed to. Both your right hand tosses will go across, you'll catch them, and then...chaos. The whole thing will fall apart because you'll try to throw the next one over there too. Meanwhile, your partner's going through the same thing. Mass confusion.

It's another psychological problem. You're in the habit of keeping all your tosses to yourself. You break it for one toss over to your partner, and then...you can't get back into the old rut, and you panic.

As usual, the cure is practice. If you're not too proud to go backwards, exercise No. 2, described above, is the least painful way to get it.

There will come a time, perhaps even in your lifetime, when you'll be able to execute this passing trick with a certain amount of flair. Repeatedly, even.

This then, is the time for graduation ceremonies. Instead of just tossing across to your partner on every third throw, toss **every** right hand bag across—while he does the same. Magnificent.

There are variations on this of course. You can each whistle the same tune. A different tune. He can talk. You can talk. You can memorize poems. Abbott and Costello had a two part routine called "Who's on first?" It takes about ten minutes. If you and your partner are able to recite this routine while team juggling, send me your address. I will fly there immediately.

CIRCLE JUGGLING

My own first, misguided attempts at juggling took this circular form where the objects follow one another around in one direction. Back in those days I never could get it, but a great deal of fruit and occasionally eggs went down in the effort.

Probably the most frustrating part of circle juggling is the fact that it is harder to learn than normal style juggling; but after you finally get it, it looks easier — so you don't get any credit for having gone through all that pain. The problem is that, in circle juggling, you have to keep two things in the air at once — (as per the diagram), but it looks as if there's only one. In regular juggling, the exact opposite is the case.

Anyway, so much for the editorial. The diagrams should give you a pretty good picture of how to do it. You'll start with two bags in your "best" hand — be it right or left — then toss them both up in quick succession in identical arcs heading over to your other hand. As soon as you've cleared your good hand, you'll have to cross the third bag into it in a quick, underneath throw.

Then all you have to do is keep everybody going around in a circle.

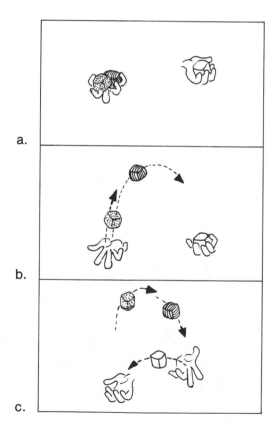

a.

b.

c.

OVERHAND GRABBING

This is just another way to make your catches. Instead of passively letting a bag land in your hand, reach up and grab it with an overhand motion. Then resume your normal juggling routine.

When you can do this consistently with either hand, you can try to toss from that overhand position (a more difficult venture). To make the toss after you have grabbed a bag, don't turn your hand back over — keep your palm down. Then flick your wrist upward, releasing the bag. This will leave your hand in a position to grab that next bag. If you can do this with every toss, you'll not only be fairly good, but you'll also have the appearance of practicing the high-speed dog paddle — which is pretty strange behavior. But by this time your friends should be used to anything.

OUTSIDE JUGGLING

This is clearly a case where a diagram is worth far more than all of my wordiness. Just look at the picture and concentrate on keeping all your tosses soft.

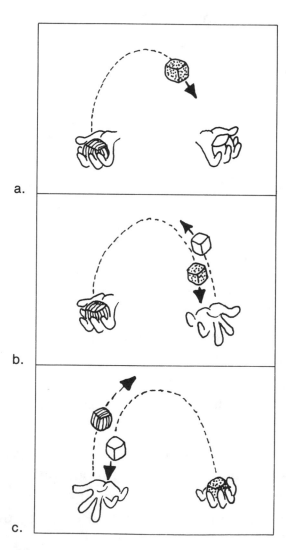

a.

b.

c.

THE "BLIND" JUGGLER

This is the most interesting trick of the lot but I include it with some reluctance because it requires one very quick handed juggler, and since quick handedness and klutziness are not often associated, this might create a problem.

Nevertheless, it's such a different kind of trick that I couldn't resist.

Stand face to face with your partner about two or three feet away. One of you is going to have to be the quick handed one while the other can be a seriously klutzy type. Settle it among yourselves as to who's who. The rest of my comments, though, will be directed to he of the quick hands.

The klutz will be the "blind" juggler, so he should close his eyes and then begin to juggle, just as if his eyes were open. But as the first bag leaves his hand, your job is to intercept it at the top of its arc and then manually (and quickly!) place it in his other hand just as he's releasing his second bag. You'll catch that one with *your* other hand and repeat the "manual exchange" in your *partner's* other hand.

The whole picture should look like this: your partner—eyes closed—will be juggling, but you'll be catching his every throw and *putting* them in his hands, right in beat with a normal juggling pattern.

The big problem is staying up with your partner and also getting your hands out of the way as his throws come up. Not easy, I admit, but still—an interesting trick.

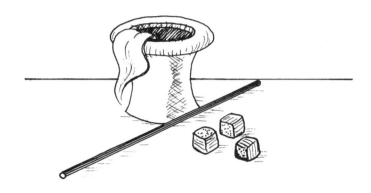

RAZZLE DAZZLE

This is the category of pure flash. Things like making one toss from behind your back, or under your leg. Or catching your final bag by stooping over and letting it land on the back of your neck. Another one consists of popping a bag up with your knee or foot rather than doing a normal exchange.

Specific directions for all these would read like an anatomy textbook and besides, they probably wouldn't be very helpful anyway.

My only hint, if you are looking to put a little of this kind of flash in your routine, is to always heave one bag especially high before you go into whatever contortions you have in mind. You can buy yourself some needed extra time with the additional height.

TWO-IN-ONE PATTERNS

This is an entirely different way to keep three objects juggled and requires that you learn how to keep two things in the air with only one hand.

It takes some time before you can do this with any kind of consistency, so you should concentrate on learning it in the hand that you're best with. If it seems harder than normal juggling, that's because it is.

At least while you're learning, you should always keep your throws going to the inside of the bag that's dropping down. This creates a kind of circular pattern. Check the diagram carefully. Unfortunately, there aren't any secrets to learning this technique — just spread it out so you don't feel overly frustrated at any one time.

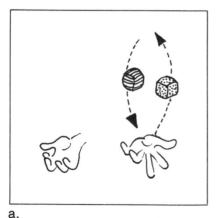
a.

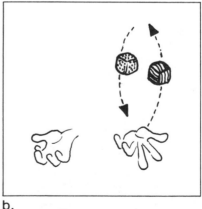
b.

Notice that the bags are going in a circular kind of pattern.

49

After you feel relatively comfortable keeping two objects juggled like this, then you can bring the third bag and your other hand into the act by just tossing it up and down in time.

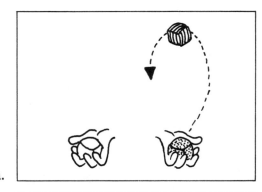

a.

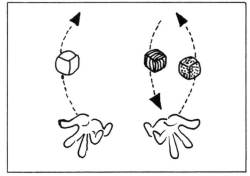

b.

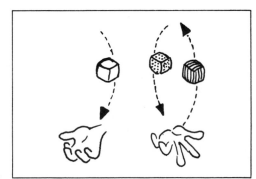

c.

NOTE: You can fake this pattern by keeping a hold — and never letting go — of the third bag. Then lift it and bring it down in time. Very cute.

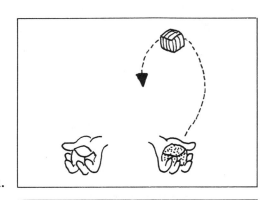

a.

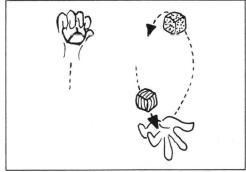

b.

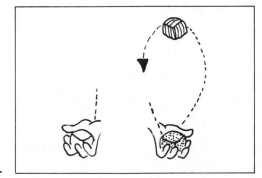

c.

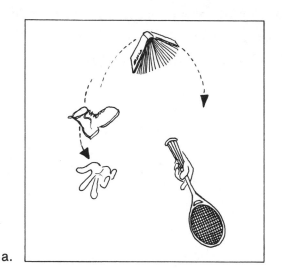

a.

JUGGLING WITH VARIOUS OBJECTS

This has always been my strongest suit, and I consider myself a near expert on the kinds of things that can be juggled.

First of all, the obvious, balls. My main hesitation about balls is that they are fine enough for juggling, but very bad for dropping. And since dropping is always a big part of my act, I have trouble with balls rolling under the furniture, dropping down storm drains, etc. Performing jugglers favor hard rubber lacrosse balls; they're expensive, but they are great for tricks where you have to bounce them off the floor rather than simply tossing them between your hands.

The diagram should give you a good idea of what's supposed to happen.

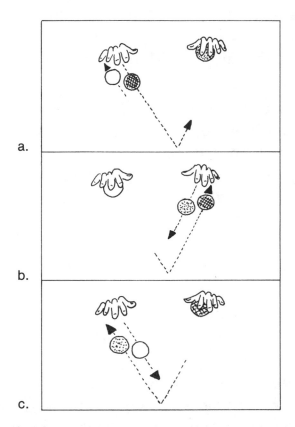

a.

b.

c.

CAUTION: If you live in a second story apartment, you probably ought to skip this one.

EDIBLES

For a beginning juggler, the produce department of any grocery store can take on a wonderful new dimension. My own favorite is the bananas. They're difficult to get the hang of at first, but even a little practice pays off quickly. If you don't try to flip them end for end, you'll find it easier.

After bananas of course there's apples, oranges, pears (when they're in season), even cantaloupes—although the weight here can be a problem.

Grapes are especially good because you can wrap up your little act by throwing them all high in the air and then catching them in your mouth. Depending on age group and interests, this can be very impressive to the person you're shopping with.

Along the same lines is the "eat-the-apple-trick" which is another great one for audience response.

Step One: Keep a careful eye out for grocery clerks.

Step Two: Take three apples and begin juggling them normally. It helps if one of them is green and the other two are red.

Step Three: When the green one gets to your right hand, make a special effort to throw it high in the air—say, about three or four feet. Keep it within reason though or you'll be visible from the next aisle.

Step Four: With the extra time you've got, bring your left-hand apple up and grab a bite out of it. If you're quick enough, you can get your hand (with bitten apple) back in place in time for the high flier to land there. You'll do an exchange and then continue juggling.

As I say, very impressive.

CAUTION: This can be a pretty messy trick, so you probably ought to dress accordingly. Also, if you don't want to eat the stem, you should twist it off at the beginning since you'll be too busy once you get started.

Just because you're out of the produce section doesn't mean there isn't anything left in the store to juggle with, but I won't list them all tediously and rob you of the pleasure of discovery.

EXCEPTION: Eggs. This is a controversial subject because drops are especially hard to recover from gracefully; but, at the same time, you don't have the roll-away problem. Use your own judgement here.

JUGGLING PINS

Performing jugglers are particularly fond of juggling pins because they look so impressive and are also easily visible from the back of the hall.

Fortunately for the rest of us, they're not nearly as tricky as they seem. Their weight, in fact, is an advantage to catching them since your fingers tend to collapse naturally around an object that slaps down heavily into your palm.

You can either make juggling pins at home, or buy them directly through the mail. The ordering information is in the back of the book.

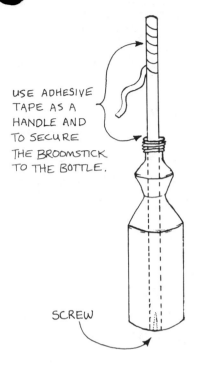

USE ADHESIVE
TAPE AS A
HANDLE AND
TO SECURE
THE BROOMSTICK
TO THE BOTTLE.

SCREW

The ingredients for home-made juggling pins are: three, old, plastic, one quart bleach bottles and three cut-off pieces of a wooden broomstick. The diagram should show you how to put them all together.

THE FLIP

Using pins to juggle with requires that you establish "the flip" solidly inside your memory banks.

Start with one pin. Hold it as per the diagram. Flip it once over to your other hand where you should catch it around the neck, just as you were holding it before. Flip it back.

Obviously this is going to be a boring exercise, but I can't think of any way around it. Practice is the only way to get it down.

After you can flip one pin back and forth, start working on an exchange with two. Practice this until it looks fairly smooth in both hands. (I'm going a little quickly over the steps here because they are identical really, except for the flip, to the steps on juggling with bean bags.)

When you can do an exchange with both hands, then you're ready for three. You'll find getting started with three is a bit awkward because there doesn't seem to be room in one hand for two juggling pins. It **is** possible though.

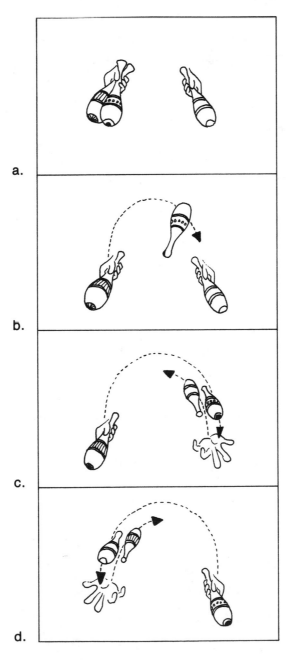

a.

b.

c.

d.

59

TRICKS WITH PINS

Once you can juggle normally with three pins, the best tricks are team tricks. Passing and stealing. The instructions for doing them are so exactly similar to the instructions I've already given for tricks with bean bags, that it seems unnecessary to repeat them. The key is, again, learning that flip to the point where it's second nature.

Individual style tricks with pins are also almost exactly parallel to those described for bean bags and the instructions can be read for either. There is, however, an additional element of risk since clonking your head with a flying juggling pin feels significantly different from the same experience with a bean bag.

I have been told that an old football helmet with face guard can solve the problem, but the image of me hitting myself on the top of my football helmet with juggling pins has kept me from pursuing the idea any further. Pride, I guess.

JUGGLING WITH FOUR

So you can juggle with three bean bags with casual flair ("So what?" I hear your friends saying). You can do two-in-one patterns with insolent ease. You even feel a certain sense of pride and accomplishment. You are, after all, a klutz on the verge of making good.

But something's missing, isn't it? You want to do four.

Before you read on, I want to warn you, while there is still time to go back. Suppose you do learn how to do four. Then what? Five? Six? It's a path to madness, and I would be remiss not to tell you that.

Despite these warnings, I know there are those among you who will still want to know how these things are done. It is for their sakes, and with some reluctance, that I set these directions down.

In order to juggle with four, you will have to develop your "off" hand in the same way that you developed your "good" hand for the two-in-one patterns. If you're right handed, that means you'll be working with your left — and vice versa.

Clearly, this is going to take some time. Your object is to keep two bean bags juggled with only one hand (your "off" hand) and do it under control.

If you can get over that hurdle, then you'll have reached the point of no return, so I might as well play the rest of this out.

A. Put two bags in each hand. Practice for a moment keeping the two in your right hand going.

B. Then stop and practice with your left.

C. Then (deep breath) practice with both hands simultaneously. You do **not** cross any bags between hands.

NOTE: Don't *start* with both hands simultaneously. Stagger your starts one...two. This is a bit hard to describe, but the idea is that your hands will be going up and down and making exchanges alternately rather than simultaneously.

A.

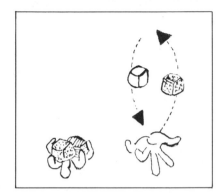

B.

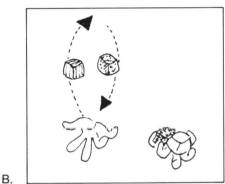

C.

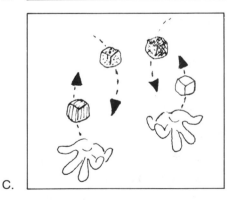

JUGGLING WITH FIVE

On a scale of one to ten, learning how to juggle with three things is a two. Learning how to juggle with four is a five. Learning how to juggle with five is a thirty-four.

If you're still interested, you're a hopeless case. I'll give you the steps to take but I disavow any further responsibility.

Put the three bags in one hand, and the remaining two in your other. Stand over a big bed. Starting with your three bag hand, toss one up in a high, perfectly accurate arc over to your other hand. But before it even peaks out, toss one out of your other hand in another perfectly accurate arc. And then (are you still there?) toss the second bag out of your first hand.

So, if we freeze the action for a second here, this is what it looks like. There are three things in the air— all perfectly thrown on arcs that pass one another, but are nevertheless **identical** in terms of height and width. Their arrangement over your hands

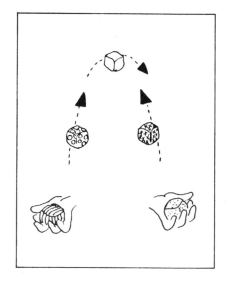

should be as illustrated. Two bags are still being held.

Now, as each flying bag drops into your hand, you'll exchange it with the flier — and in this way (theoretically) you should be able to keep everything going.

The pattern used in juggling with five is the same pattern used in juggling with three. The minor difference being that there are now three things in the air instead of one.

Incidentally, the first three tosses should all leave your hand about as quickly as you can say, "one toss, two toss, three toss". The only sort of exercise I know of that might help is to begin with three bags. Throw them all up in this quick sequence kind of way. Your hands should then be momentarily empty before you begin catching and going back into a normal juggling routine.

This would be a good trick to learn if you ever get a job on a desert island or in a lighthouse.

THE OUTER FRINGE

If you're waiting for me to talk about juggling with flying hatchets, knives, and flaming torches, you can forget it. One part of me recognizes that these things are in reality no more difficult than juggling pins — assuming they're properly weighted — but the other part of me knows better, a lot better, in fact.

I have, in my own small way, found an appropriate substitute for these things and I will pass along my little discovery to you.

A plumber's helper. One of those big rubber suction things. Not as flashy as a flaming torch, maybe, but still, I think it has a little charm of its own. Anyway, there it is — you can take it or leave it.

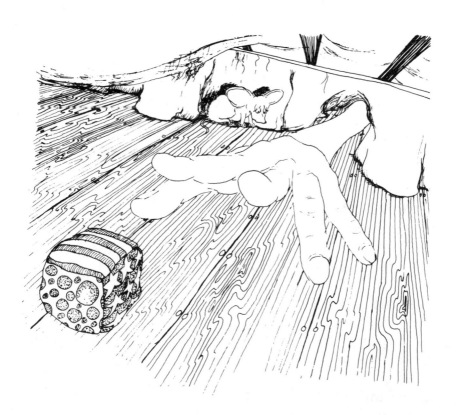

ORDERING INFORMATION

JUGGLING BAGS
- They don't bounce around, they don't roll away, and they won't make a mess on the floor.
- Three colorful, hand-sewn bean bags of calico and denim . . . ideal size and weight for juggling.

ULTIMATE JUGGLING BAGS
- Sewn with crushed red velour (instead of calico and denim). Appropriate for most formal occasions.

JUGGLING RINGS
- Three colorful ABS plastic juggling rings (outside diameter 13", inside diameter 11-1/2", 3/16" thick). Sergei Ignatov, the Reggie Jackson of juggling, always uses rings when keeping more than 11 objects going at once.

JUGGLING FOR THE COMPLETE KLUTZ
- The most popular book on juggling ever published.

THE SET
- *Juggling for the Complete Klutz* plus three juggling bags.

JUGGLING PINS
- Three white, injection molded polyethylene juggling pins. They're completely indestructible, and they won't hurt your head like bowling pins will.

JUGGLING BALLS
- Three lacrosse-style, hard rubber balls with a ribbed, easy-to-grip surface. Each set contains one red, one blue and one yellow ball.

PROFESSIONAL STYLE PINS
- For the semi-serious juggler. Polyethylene construction, with a padded knob, bottom, extra length cushioned handle, and a two-tone gold and white finish. Barnum and Bailey material.

ORDERING BLANKS

Please indicate items ordered and enclose full amount in check or money order. All prices shown are postpaid.

☒ Juggling Bags ___*3*___ (qty.) *$2.00 each ($5.00 for three)*
☐ *Ultimate* Juggling Bags _____ set(s) (available only
   in sets of 3) *$7.50 per set*
☐ *Juggling for the Complete Klutz* _____ (qty.) *$4.50 each*
☐ The Set *(one book plus three bean bags)* _____ (qty.)
   $10.50 each.
☐ Juggling Pins _____ set(s) *$21.50 for each set of three.*
☐ Professional Style Pins _____ set(s) *$47.50 for each set of
   three.*
☐ Juggling Rings _____ set(s) *$22.50 for each set of three.*
☐ Juggling Balls _____ set(s) *$8.50 per set.*

Name _____

Street _____

City _____

State/Zip _____

☐ Juggling Bags _____ (qty.) *$2.50 each ($5.00 for three)*
☐ *Ultimate* Juggling Bags _____ set(s) (available only
   in sets of 3) *$7.50 per set*
☐ *Juggling for the Complete Klutz* _____ (qty.) *$4.50 each*
☐ The Set *(one book plus three bean bags)* _____ (qty.)
   $10.50 each.
☐ Juggling Pins _____ set(s) *$21.50 for each set of three.*
☐ Professional Style Pins _____ set(s) *$47.50 for each set of
   three.*
☐ Juggling Rings _____ set(s) *$22.50 for each set of three.*
☐ Juggling Balls _____ set(s) *$8.50 per set.*

Name _____

Street _____

City _____

State/Zip _____

Send to:
Klutz Enterprises/P.O.Box 2992/Stanford, CA 94305